Table of Contents

Introduction

What Is a Growth Mindset?

Growth mindset, identified by Carol Dweck[1], is the belief that your intelligence or ability is malleable and that with practice and effort, you can "get smarter." People with growth mindsets embrace challenges, learn from mistakes, persist, and view effort as a necessary and integral part of learning. Characteristics associated with people with growth mindsets include grit, perseverance, and tenacity—the ability or drive to continue toward a goal even when it's difficult. People with growth mindsets are likely to seek out help and to share their thinking with others. They also tend to have a better sense of self-efficacy and autonomy because they believe that their efforts and mistakes are part of learning and improvement and because they know that they have control over their successes and failures. Understandably, people with growth mindsets tend to be intrinsically motivated.

A fixed mindset, on the other hand, stands in contrast to a growth mindset. People with fixed mindsets believe their intelligence is fixed—they are either smart or not smart, a good athlete or not a good athlete. They are concerned with the way they look to others and often shy away from challenges. They feel effort is a sign of weakness or a waste of time and are at times resentful of others who succeed. People with fixed mindsets tend to be extrinsically motivated and focused on performance, completing tasks to be recognized or receive awards. Research shows that students with growth mindsets approach challenges with enthusiasm, take risks when learning, and persevere[2]. As such, it behooves educators to support growth mindsets in the classroom.

Mindsets in the Classroom

Most articles and research about supporting growth mindsets in the classroom are about teaching students about the brain[3], and about the type of language teachers use in the classroom[4]. Research demonstrates that shifting language usage when providing feedback can greatly impact how students approach, perform, and later discuss challenging tasks[5]. Therefore, let's take a closer look at the specific language that either supports or stifles a growth mindset.

Mindsets develop from a person interacting with his or her environment, including how success and failure are perceived. If the language in the classroom connotes success and failure as reflections of a person's ability, fixed mindsets thrive. However, if the language in the classroom portrays success and failure as reflections of a person's effort or perseverance, growth mindsets thrive.

For example, person-oriented praise or criticism tends to promote fixed mindsets. Comments like, "You are so smart," "You are such a good artist," or "Math isn't your best subject, so just try," negatively impact students' beliefs in their abilities because the comments are judgments and personal. They have a sense of finality to them.

On the other hand, process-oriented feedback tends to promote growth mindsets. Comments that focus on the process or choices a student makes put the student's actions at the forefront. For example, "That seemed easy to you. Let's try something more challenging," or "This problem is difficult, but with some more practice and patience, you'll get it," or "This problem is difficult. I see you've tried one strategy and it's not working. What else could you try?" Process comments support student autonomy and agency because they place the focus on the learner's choices. Many studies show how impactful the addition of one word, "yet," can be in shaping a growth mindset.

For example, "You don't understand that *yet*. The inclusion of *yet* expresses that learning is a process and that, with time and effort, you will get there.

Using and believing in the word "yet" and normalizing challenges, struggle, and mistakes is especially supportive of students learning a language or students with learning challenges.

However, not all process-oriented feedback is created equal. One component of providing growth mindset comments is taking "I like" or "I love" out of the feedback. Many teachers begin their comments with "I like the way," or "I love the way." But feedback should not be about what the teacher likes. It should be about what the student did or did not do, what the student understands or doesn't understand. "I like" is a judgment that implicitly sends the message that a student is learning to please the teacher. When process-oriented feedback begins with "I like" or "I love," it promotes a fixed mindset because the focus shifts from the process to a judgment. The "I like" turns the comment into a form of praise, promoting a performance-driven situation, which will likely lead the student to seek external rewards.

The use of the phrase "thank you" also sends the implicit message that a student is learning for someone else. Comments meant to encourage or compliment, like "Thank you for completing the assignment," or "Thank you for putting forth so much effort," actually support the idea that students are not learning for themselves but are learning or behaving to please the teacher—and therefore, they are learning for some external reward, which, again, supports a fixed mindset. Similarly, when a teacher says, "Write a response to your reading *for me*," the *for me* sends the message that a student's completion of tasks in school are done for the teacher, rather than for the student himself or herself.

Furthermore, making judgments, even positive ones, like "good job" or "excellent," focuses on performance. Responding to a student without judgment, either by actively listening and repeating back what the student says or by asking questions of clarification, supports student's developing autonomy and agency. For example, when a student who has difficulty with multi-step math problems shows his teacher that he solved the problem correctly, the teacher could say, "Nice job," or "Well done," which praises the student for getting the correct answer. However, the praise does not address his effort, his process, or his learning. In fact, the praise stops his learning. Instead, the teacher could ask the student, "How did you do it?" With this response, the student has the opportunity to explain his process and reflect on the choices he made. His recounting of his process deepens his understanding, so his learning continues. By providing feedback instead of praise, a growth mindset can be fostered, supporting students' independence, ability to make choices, and motivation to accomplish tasks that were originally difficult.

Growth mindset comments are truthful and specific. They're not about praise—praise is judgmental. Since feedback that promotes a growth mindset tends to focus on process, many comments that promote a growth mindset do the following:

- name what the student is doing
- state why/how what the student is doing is helpful to learning
- offer direction for moving on or for more practice
- leave the teacher out of the commentary (no judgments)
- include language that explicitly and implicitly supports practice, growth, and development (*Yet*, *What else could you try?*, *Learning takes time*, etc.).

It's More Than Language

While research has shown that certain language promotes fixed mindsets and certain language promotes growth mindsets, it is not all about language. The space, the time, and the way instruction is organized also impact students' beliefs about themselves as learners. Classrooms that support a growth mindset are organized to support student choice, ownership, and autonomy. Teachers pay attention to how materials are arranged, the structure of assignments, when to provide feedback, and what type of language to use. Moreover, explicitly teaching students about the brain and how it develops when challenged or when mistakes are made has been found to support the understanding, internalization, and development of a growth mindset.

In addition to language, other aspects of a classroom are important in supporting a growth mindset. For example:

- **Space** is organized to foster independence and autonomy. The classroom space belongs to students. They access materials when needed and they take pride in what the classroom looks like.

- **Time** is fluid. Students are provided time to think, examine, and redo. There is time for reflection and metacognition, to make mistakes, and to put forth effort to see results. Learning is not rushed or confined to a 45-minute block. While many schools operate within 45-minute periods, teachers can organize learning experiences that cross over days or weeks. In addition, teachers can also integrate learning and teach content (reading, writing, math) across the curriculum.

Teaching across content areas is not possible in all schools. But teachers who work in schools that allow cross-curricular instruction should try teaming up with another teacher in the grade or speak with the principal about scheduling longer blocks of time. If neither option is possible, be sure to provide ample opportunities to work through the process of learning and reflection.

- **Management** is cooperative, not competitive. It is not about who finishes first. Rather, it is about how we can all come to understand.

- **Instruction** is open-ended, authentic, purposeful, and challenging. Part of instruction includes planning experiences for students in which they have opportunities to make choices and take ownership of their learning. It's also about allowing students to struggle and grapple with big ideas. Furthermore, even after careful planning, teachers should be open to spontaneity and willing to engage in new questions and explorations that might not have been planned.

- **Mistakes** are examined to support learning or to deepen understanding.

The way teachers organize the classroom space and their time sends different messages—either "I'm in control and this is my classroom" or "We're in control and this is our classroom." The latter stance promotes a growth mindset. When students have a say in organizing their space, they feel that they are in control of their own learning and that they can continue to grow.

Joint Construction of Space

- **Include students in labeling and organizing the library.**
- **Discuss with students about where materials could be housed and the best way to access them.**
- **Encourage students to label centers and other parts of the room themselves.**
- **Document student process and progress on the walls (including drafts and what was learned from mistakes).**
- **Document growth mindset comments, characteristics, and behaviors.**
- **Create different areas in the classroom to support different types of learners.**

The items listed above will be more difficult to execute than others for teachers who teach multiple classes in the same room. Try to be flexible and think of ways to engage students so they feel some ownership of the classroom.

A Teacher's Mindset

A teacher's beliefs about success and failure can also greatly impact a student's mindset. A teacher who exhibits a fixed mindset might find it difficult to orchestrate a classroom environment that supports a growth mindset. Therefore, it's important for teachers to take a step back to think about their own beliefs, not only about students but about themselves. It's even important for teachers to reflect on the language they use, including their internal talk, to describe themselves.

Below are some questions teachers can ask themselves to begin thinking about their own mindset.

- What do I do when I am faced with a challenge?
- In what situations am I comfortable to take risks?
- In what situations am I not comfortable to take risks?
- What do I do when I'm learning something new? How do I feel throughout the process?
- How do I describe myself with regards to things that might not be strengths?

Next, teachers can reflect on their teaching.

- How do I encourage risk-taking in the classroom?
- How do I provide opportunities for all students to learn?
- In what ways do I support students who need more time?
- What structures are in place to support effort and perseverance?
- What's my management system?
- How are materials accessed?

Finally, teachers can:

- Record themselves teaching: What type of language am I using?
- Examine their unit plans: What mindset do the lessons, goals, and objectives promote? How about the structure of the unit?
- Examine their management routines: Who's in control?
- Think about ways to align their beliefs about students and learning with what is happening in the classroom.

Reflecting on one's own mindset can be challenging and takes time. It may help to work with a colleague. Remember, it's a process. For the most part, in our own lives and in our classrooms, we do not exhibit one mindset all the time; there is a continuum—and where we fall on that continuum is based on many factors. Therefore, some aspects of the classroom may support the development of growth mindsets, while others might promote more fixed mindsets.

Ideas to Infuse a Growth Mindset

Below are some ideas that can easily be implemented to infuse a growth mindset into your classroom.

Observe

Teachers can observe students to better understand their mindsets, then think of ways to support or strengthen growth mindset characteristics or behaviors. For example, teachers can ask the following questions and then chart their findings.

1. What is the student doing? (Note specific behaviors.)
2. How does the student talk about his/her work or learning? (Document words/phrases.)
3. What mindset do you think the behavior and language demonstrate?
4. What types of comments/structures might support this student?

Use Models

One way to illustrate a growth mindset in the classroom is to engage in conversations about characters in books or famous people in the content area. Find biographies or videos in which people talk about their journeys. Most people's journeys are fraught with dead-ends and disappointment. But what got them to where they are was honing their craft and not giving up. If students know the terminology and descriptors of growth mindsets because the attributes have been openly pointed out and discussed during reading, they will be more likely to internalize a growth mindset themselves. Learning how others have dealt with challenges illustrates to students how they, too, can deal with setbacks.

Teach About the Brain

Another way to introduce mindsets and the value of challenge, perseverance, and making mistakes is to teach students about how the brain works and develops. In the beginning of the year, have students study the brain so they can learn about how it grows stronger. There are many online videos and a few programs that specifically teach students about their brain and its relationship to having a growth mindset or a fixed mindset. The most widely known, developed with Carol Dweck, is Brainology[6], a web-based program.

A Word About Behavior Management Systems

Many classrooms have color systems or ticket systems to "manage" behavior. These behavior modification systems are really about controlling students' behavior and create tension for teachers trying to encourage and support growth mindsets[7]. Color or ticket systems are quite arbitrary, as there is no way a teacher can possibly "catch" every behavior and identify its root. Imagine a student who tries to answer a friend's question about the work (the teacher said students were supposed to help each other). When the student talks to help her friend, the teacher moves her from green to yellow. When she tries to explain she was helping her friend, the teacher takes 5 minutes off recess. The teacher was focused on controlling behavior, but was never aware of why the student was talking. Another problem with color and ticket systems is that they usually leave little room for student reflection. The color is changed or the ticket is removed, and that is the end of it. Some teachers say students can "earn tickets back" (have them removed), but rarely discuss how that might occur or provide supports for students to regulate their own behavior. And again, it would be the choice of the teacher if the student "earned" the ticket back, which depends on whether the teacher "catches" the student doing the right thing. These systems send the implicit message that students can't be trusted, which is contrary to a classroom where growth mindset is fostered. Creating a classroom culture of mutual respect, one where students reflect on their learning and the behaviors that support their learning, tends to support the development of growth mindsets.

Using This Book

This book is organized so teachers can dip in and out of it, accessing just what they need in the moment. There are sections for each content area, as well as sections for management, whole-class instruction, prompts for students, and working with parents. Each section contains a brief overview of the specific topic and growth mindset comments. Remember, supporting a growth mindset is a confluence of managing time, space, instruction, and language in the classroom.

General Comments

The comments are organized into five categories that relate to the main tenets of a growth mindset. Although the categories are not completely discrete, this organization provides a structure for teachers to focus on different aspects of a growth mindset based on a student's individual needs. For example, if a student would benefit from support in making his or her own choices in math, comments in the "Autonomy" section may be most helpful.

- **Effort/Resilience:** These comments support students' effort and ability to continue trying, even when mistakes are made. The intention of these comments is to acknowledge that challenge and effort support learning and reaching goals.
- **Autonomy:** These comments provide students with the opportunity to make choices about their learning.
- **Reflection/Metacognition:** Since part of developing a growth mindset is the ability to reflect on past learning experiences, these comments remind students to think about past learning or challenges to inform how to address new challenges or rethink what they are doing in the moment.
- **Collaboration:** Part of supporting a growth mindset classroom includes working together, which means grappling with challenges and sharing successes, as well as reaching out for help.
- **Cross-Over:** Comments that can fit into more than one category.

Nurturing a growth mindset is more complex than selecting the "right" comments. This book is intended to help teachers internalize not only the language of a growth mindset, but also the importance of management and planning in fostering a growth mindset.

Classroom Management

Classroom management shouldn't be about control. It should be about trust and engagement. In classrooms that support a growth mindset, students feel ownership in the classroom and engage in ways to make classroom management better. The structures teachers set up, often in collaboration with students, can help support a growth mindset when the structures come from a place of trust and are scaffolded for those who need it. What is equally important is the language teachers use within the context of transitions and learning. Remember, if teachers say things like, "I like how Johnny is sitting" or "I love the way Amy raised her hand," they are promoting a performance-based, judgment-filled classroom. What if other students were also sitting and ready, or also raised their hands, but weren't recognized? Next time, they might not engage, especially if they are doing it for the external praise.

In addition, providing space and time in the classroom for students to revise or redo their work, not as a punishment but as an opportunity to improve and learn, supports the growth mindset. When students are given the opportunity to revise, there's an implicit belief that students are capable and are held to high expectations—some students may just need more time. However, simply handing the work back and telling the student to do it over will not develop learning or a growth mindset. Feedback and support must be provided so students can learn from the revision and extra time. Having students redo or retry something normalizes struggle, and encourages the idea that learning is a process. Here are some comments that promote the kind of classroom management that fosters a growth mindset.

Effort/ Resilience

- We definitely need more practice.
- A bit challenging—yes?
- What happens to the brain when you keep trying?
- I think some people need more time.

Autonomy

- It's your choice.
- I see you made a plan for yourself.
- When you are ready for a more difficult text, what can you do?
- What can you do when you are finished?
- How might you extend your learning?

Reflection/ Metacognition

- Think about how you supported your group today.
- Write down ways in which you took risks today.
- If you could, what would you like to redo today?
- What did you do today that you are proud of?
- Were you ready and prepared today? If not, what will you do tomorrow to ensure that you are ready and prepared? If you were, how can you replicate that?

Collaboration

- How can we solve this problem together?
- Let's think of ways to organize the library.
- Let's see what we can learn from looking at the different ideas.
- Let's develop some rules (or routines) for group work so everyone can learn.

Cross-Over

- I've noticed that some students didn't quite understand the ______ (insert skill or concept or content) introduced yesterday. If you had difficulty, I'll be conducting a review session for the first 15 minutes of independent work time. If you think you need more practice or more explanation, ______ (Explain what students can do: go to the back table, arrange a conference with the teacher or a partner, etc.).
- Remember to write how you solved the problem. That way you'll get better at pinpointing where you might have made a mistake and, therefore, will be better able to correct it.
- Controlling our behavior can be difficult, especially when we are excited or frustrated. Let's work together to come up with some strategies to use so our excitement or frustration doesn't stop us from learning.
- Choose a partner you think you can work well with.
- Choose a partner you think will challenge you.

These comments do not call out individual students with praise statements, such as "I like." Instead, they focus on the process. If there are one or two students in the class who are consistently not ready, pull them aside and discuss ways to support them in being ready and open to learning.

Whole-Class Discussions

Teaching is more than delivering content. When working with students, teachers also aspire to teach students about themselves as learners—how they can develop a voice and sense of belonging in a community of learners. As such, teaching in a whole-class setting provides ample opportunities to model growth mindset behaviors and thinking, including agency, autonomy, self-confidence, and a love of learning. When possible, ask questions that can be answered in more than one way. For example, instead of asking, *How is the character feeling?,* try *How **might** the character be feeling?* The slight change in the question supports students' individual thinking and encourages explanation and discussion of ideas because the question suggests more than one right answer. The way teachers frame their lessons and the way they respond to students matters. Remember, also, to refrain from placing judgments on students' comments, like "good" or "excellent." Below are some growth mindset comments teachers might say during whole-class lessons/discussions. Many of the comments can also be used when working with individual students or small groups.

Effort/ Resilience

- Don't understand it yet? We'll have to practice some more.
- Still not clear? Let's try it a different way.
- This is challenging material, but with practice and perseverance, we'll get it.
- Remember the feeling you had once you finally solved that problem.
- This concept is challenging, but think about how we'll feel once you figure it out.

Autonomy

In a whole-class lesson, autonomy can be tricky. To promote autonomy in whole-class lessons, have students talk amongst themselves and interact on their own, instead of through the teacher. In a whole-class discussion that supports autonomy, the teacher would be a member of the discussion or a facilitator but not the central participant.

- Remember that you are talking to each other.
- We're building our understanding together, so listen to what each person is saying.
- How might someone build on ______'s (student) idea?
- Which of the points discussed do you think we should continue to explore?
- Before we begin the discussion, think about how you might contribute.
- Let's take 5 minutes to prepare for the discussion. Look over your notes.

Reflection/ Metacognition

- Let's look at our progress.
- Explain your process so others might learn from it.
- How has your thinking changed?
- Yesterday we learned ______. Take a minute to write down what you remember and what you still have questions about.
- What strategies have you used that help you contribute to discussions?

Collaboration

- Can someone help clarify?
- During small-group work, I worked with ______ (student) and ______ (student). They're going to share a mistake they made so we can learn from it.
- With your partner, write a summary sentence about what just happened in the chapter. Write it on a sticky note.
- Sometimes, we learn more when we work together because our ideas are challenged.
- Questions that get us thinking help clarify our ideas.

Cross-Over

- I'm not sure I understand what you mean. Think about it a bit more. When you're ready, we'll come back to you.
- It seems like we're a bit confused. Let's step back for a moment. On your own, go through your notebook and take a look at some of the articles. Then write down two questions you have that might clarify our understanding.
- Now that we all have a clear understanding, how can we build on that understanding to challenge ourselves?
- How has your thinking changed based on other people's comments or what I just modeled?
- Think about two strategies you've used that have been helpful and write them on your sticky note. Then think about one strategy you have not yet used. We'll share that one strategy in a "whip around." If the opportunity presents itself today, challenge yourself to use that strategy.

These comments are important on their own, but equally important is how they are embedded within the larger context of the classroom. The way teachers organize their time and instruction matters, too.

Whip Around

A "whip around" is when each person in a group says something without any comments from others. It is a quick way to get a sense of students' thinking and a sense of the class as a whole. This can be done for many topics, including: pulling quotes from texts, strategies used to solve math problems, remaining questions, etc. One of the many benefits is that everyone speaks, so each student's voice is equal. Since there is no discussion, there is no judgment.

Prompts for Students' Self-Talk

Language, classroom management, and instruction all play a part in supporting the development of growth mindsets. However, another integral piece includes providing students with prompts for self-talk and questioning. As part of supporting students' autonomy and control of their learning, it is also helpful for students to engage in goal setting and to track their development as they reach their goals. It is important to provide time and scaffolds—such as the self-talk comments below–so students can do that. Since the comments provide different entry points into growth mindset thinking, rather than presenting them all at once, choose which ones to introduce based on individual and class needs.

Effort/ Resilience

- I need more time to think this through.
- I am worthy of a challenge.
- Everyone makes mistakes.
- Mistakes help me learn.
- I don't understand this yet.
- If I practice, I will get better.
- This is difficult. It might take me some time to understand.
- This is difficult, but I can use it as an opportunity to learn.
- If something is difficult but I stick with it, my brain will grow and I will learn.
- This is difficult, but I can use what I know to work through it.
- With perseverance, I will overcome this challenge.

Autonomy

- I am in control of my learning.
- What other ways can I approach this?
- I make choices about how I learn.
- I can always try again.
- What else could I try?
- How can I make this more challenging?

Reflection/ Metacognition

- My choices yesterday helped me stay focused. I'll try to make the same choices today.
- That didn't work. Now what?
- When I try (insert a strategy), I tend to understand. Maybe I should continue to use that strategy.
- I'm automatic with that skill now. I'll try something harder.
- Am I doing my best? How do I know?

Collaboration

- I think if we do this together, it will help both of us.
- I think I can learn from you, so can we do this together?
- I should share my ideas so others can learn from me.
- I will work with someone who challenges me.
- I will work with someone who has different strengths so I can learn from him or her.

Cross-Over

- ______ (student) might be able to do that really well. I wonder if he or she has seen this material before. Maybe I'll ask.
- This is really hard, but I have lots of strategies I can use. Last time I used ______. Maybe I'll try that. If that doesn't work, I can try ______.
- I think I should share this mistake. Others can learn from what I didn't understand.
- When I get frustrated, I won't give up. I will take a break and come back to it with fresh eyes.
- Based on what my partner said, I think I should...
- Who would be the best person to help me?

Partner and Group Conversation

When students work with partners or in groups, they should utilize growth mindset comments as well. Although the language teachers use is a powerful model for students to emulate, it is also useful to provide explicit supports for students. Below are some guidelines and prompts for partners or groups to use.

- I'm not sure I understand. Can you repeat that?
- What do you mean by that?
- Can someone else explain?
- That's what I thought, but what were you thinking?
- This is difficult, but I think if we all participate we can figure it out.
- Here's the challenge: how do we include all of our ideas into the presentation?
- I'm not sure I agree with that. Here's why...
- I agree, and...
- Yes, and...
- ______ (student), we haven't heard from you. What are your thoughts?

It's a good idea to have students reflect individually and as a group. They can also develop goals for the next time they meet. Reflecting individually and as a group and setting individual and group goals support a growth mindset because reflection and goal-setting focus on process and provide students with opportunities to improve. Doing so also promotes the idea that we are all learning and growing. Many teachers find it useful to provide reflection/goal sheets for students or prompts to guide students, at least in the beginning.

Growth Mindset: Reading Comments

Supporting a growth mindset in reading has a lot to do with how literacy instruction is organized, how teachers talk with students about reading, and how students talk with each other about reading. For example, a teacher who supports a growth mindset will celebrate and elicit multiple interpretations of texts, invite students to disagree, and expect students to support their opinions with evidence from the text or from their own experiences. In addition, reading classrooms that support a growth mindset celebrate each student's processes and development trajectory. The teacher supports, guides, facilitates, invites, and provides multiple opportunities for students to engage with and access text. Comments like the ones below put students in control of their learning.

Effort/ Resilience

- I see you haven't settled on a book yet...
- What is challenging you right now with this book/text?
- Two months ago this book was too difficult for you. Now it's not. See how practice and perseverance can help.
- Your reading will get better if you read more.
- Your reading will get better if you challenge yourself.

Autonomy

- What strategies are you using to help you keep track of all the characters?
- This topic seems quite complicated. How will you keep all the information organized?
- It seems like this book has lots of sophisticated vocabulary. How are you making sure you understand the vocabulary?
- When you came to that multisyllabic word, I noticed you looked for prefixes and suffixes and put the word together. This can be an effective strategy.
- Here are some ideas that can help you focus when you can't seem to get started:
  - –Reread the beginning of the book or the last chapter you read.
  - –Read something different, like an article, short story, or favorite picture book.
  - –Ask a few friends to suggest a book.
  - –Try reflecting on why you might not be interested in reading your books today. (Write your ideas in your notebook.)
- Which one will you try?

Asking a student which strategy he or she might try puts the choice and responsibility in his or her court. Also, note that the question is not, "Do you want to try it?" The question implies the expectation that the student will try something.

Reflection/ Metacognition

- I noticed you looked at the Table of Contents then at the glossary. What were you thinking while you were doing all of that? How does that pre-work support your reading?
- What did you do to connect the different points of view?
- You're having trouble choosing a book. Remember last month when you zipped through the ______ series? What about that series was so engaging? Maybe make a chart of the characteristics, and you can try to find a book that meets some or all of the criteria.

Collaboration

- Explain your thinking to the group to spark some conversation that will support everyone's understanding of the text.
- Why don't you share how writing about your reading led you to an "aha" moment today.
- It might be cool if you created an "If you like..., you might like..." chart for others in the class who might be having the same challenge with choosing a book.
- Talking with your partner or book group can help you understand the text in different ways.
- This group connected the different texts by their themes or big ideas. Another group connected the texts based on structure.

Cross-Over

- At times reading is difficult. Sometimes we don't understand what we've read the first time. So what can we do?
- It looks like you tried to keep track of the different ______ (story elements, author craft, unknown words, etc.) in your notebook, but then you stopped. Why?
- The character chart you've created seems to be helping you keep track of all the character connections. ______ (student) is reading a similar book with lots of characters. I think he/she would appreciate it if you explained your process to him/her.
- I noticed you've tried a few things to get started with your reading, but none seem to be working today. What other strategies might you try?

This comment supports the notion that learning feels different at different times, and just because something worked previously, doesn't mean it will work all the time. Learners need to be flexible.

Growth Mindset: Writing Comments

Writing takes time. In classrooms that support a growth mindset, students have ample opportunity to write, revise, rewrite, and edit. They also have many low-stakes opportunities to write. They write to communicate, to make sense of what they've learned, to tell stories, even to make sense of themselves and the world around them. In classrooms where a growth mindset is cultivated, students are more apt to take risks, tackling difficult topics and incorporating various text structures and craft moves into their writing. The teaching of writing is presented as a recursive process of ideas and words. Getting words on paper that say exactly what the writer wants is challenging. Supporting students to take on that challenge in a way that supports their autonomy helps foster growth mindsets. Here are some comments you might incorporate into your writing classes.

Effort/ Resilience

- So how are you challenging yourself as a writer today?
- I see you have three different beginnings. Keep working at it until you have something you are happy with.
- You seem to be erasing quite a bit today. What's giving you trouble?
- Writing is a difficult process so we have to practice all parts, even when they are difficult.
- You've worked hard on your thesis statement, and I think it has paid off. You've focused your topic so it is compelling, and as a reader I know what to expect.

Autonomy

- You mentioned earlier that you wanted to incorporate dialogue into your opening scene. What are you hoping the dialogue will add to the reader's experience?
- You're trying to create a ______ mood. What have you done so far?
- I see you've chosen a ______ web to organize your ideas.
- Remember to reread exactly what is on the page and continue to challenge yourself by making choices about how you want to tell your story. Keep in mind what you want the reader to feel and get out of the story.
- I agree that talking your idea out is one strategy that might help. You might also begin by writing notes so you can get the ideas down first and then work on the wording. Give it a try—talk your ideas out or jot down notes and see how it works.

Reflection/ Metacognition

- What strategies are you using to engage the reader?
- How might you revise your piece based on looking over your mentor text?
- Reread your piece slowly. Play close attention to the punctuation that is on the page and think about how you might revise.
- What is giving you trouble in this piece?
- What went well today?
- Did anything in your writing surprise you today?
- How would your writing piece change if the audience changed?

Collaboration

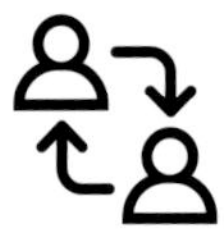

- Share your piece with your partner. No judgments. Just consider what's working for you and what's not, or places where you noticed he/she used a craft move.
- Why don't you talk with ______ (student) about that structure? She wrote a text like that a few months ago, maybe she can give you a few tips.
- Talk through your ______ (plot, argument, etc.) points with your partner. Think carefully about how clearly you are introducing your topic.
- ______ (student) is very interested in that genre/topic, too. Maybe you can write a piece together or create companion pieces.

Cross-Over

- You said you are going to change the setting. Can you explain the thinking behind that decision?
- So I noticed you have not begun writing yet. What's going on?

> **This comment states the obvious and then puts the student in control. Be sure to provide enough wait time for a response, especially if students are not used to being asked about their process.**

- Any ideas for what you could try to work through the frustration? If not, talk with ______ (student). He was having similar frustrations last week.
- This is your third draft! How has it changed from the first?
- You think your writing is going really well because you have a lot of ideas on ways to make it better, based on your partner's comments. Getting feedback from others can be a very useful strategy. I know many writers who do that.
- You've worked really hard to draw the reader in by using different craft. The dialogue not only moves the plot along, but I can get a real sense of the characters based on what they say. Your use of ______ (vivid verbs, concrete nouns, metaphors, similes, etc.) like ______ (give an example) kept me engaged.

Growth Mindset: Mathematics Comments

While much of the growth mindset thinking is the same from content area to content area, there are some content-specific ideas to keep in mind. In math, it is important to craft tasks that are open-ended and that can be solved in different ways. Many students believe that math is about computing and about getting the correct answer. And while that may be true in some instances, math is also about problem solving, which often involves finding patterns and visualizing[8]. When organizing content, try to provide opportunities for students to explain their thinking verbally and in writing, draw their thinking, and also converse—even debate with peers—about different approaches to solving a problem. Consider using the following comments to support a growth mindset in mathematics.

Effort/ Resilience

- You look frustrated. That's normal because this is challenging.
- If you continue to persevere, your brain will continue to grow.
- So you made a mistake. That's okay. Try something else.
- What did you learn from the mistake?
- This problem is a bit more challenging. Give it a try.
- How are you challenging yourself today in math?

Autonomy

- What plan have you decided upon to solve the problem?
- What does this problem remind you of? How can that help you decide where to begin?
- What might you try now?
- I see you have tried quite a few strategies and stopped. Let's develop a plan together so you use one strategy all the way through.
- What can you do if you don't know how to begin?

Reflection/ Metacognition

- What is it about this problem that stumped you?
- Can you figure out where the mistake is?
- How might you apply what you learned from this problem to others?
- I see you created a chart to keep track of the information, but then you stopped. What was your thinking?
- You don't think the answer you got is correct? How do you know?
- How might you revise your thinking?

Collaboration

- Why don't you share your thinking with your math partner?
- Ask ______ (student) about how he/she solved the problem. It might give you some ideas.
- Will you explain your mistake to the class so others can learn from it?
- With your group, come up with a pattern for others to solve. Remember to use what we know about numbers and their relationships when making the pattern.
- In your group, develop a sentence explaining the ______ [Insert mathematical concept, for example: how decimals, fractions, and percents are related, positive and negative numbers, symmetry and congruence.] based on the problems we've been working on this week

Cross-Over

- What strategy did you choose to use? How do you think that strategy will help?
- You know it's incorrect because it shouldn't be a whole number. So what should you do now?
- I've noticed that partners are working together to develop a plan for how to solve the problem. I'm hearing lots of mathematical terminology and also noticing that partners are really listening to each other. Are any partners stuck? Would you like to ask the class for some ideas?
- Let's quickly go around the room to share pairs' initial thoughts. I'll chart the ideas.

It's important to document thinking throughout a process so students can reflect on their initial thinking and their developing understandings.

- What did you notice about the way partners went about solving the problem? Notice any patterns? Does anything puzzle you?

Growth Mindset: Science Comments

How do we encourage students' natural curiosity and desire to explore and take risks? By supporting a growth mindset. Science and the growth mindset should come together seamlessly in the classroom. Unfortunately, in many classrooms, they don't. All to often, science is about following a procedure that has a right way and a wrong way, and a right and wrong answer. Many science classrooms are devoid of inquiry, mistakes, and messiness. Like the math classroom and the social studies classroom that foster a growth mindset, learning experiences in science should be open-ended. Students should have time to ask questions, make mistakes, and start again. In addition, students need to have a sense of ownership by generating their own questions and designing ways to answer them. In science classrooms that promote a growth mindset, teachers organize instruction in a way that supports mistakes, celebrates challenges, and provides opportunities for students to reflect on their work and learning. Following are some growth mindset comments teachers might use during science.

Effort/ Resilience

- What might be challenging about this?
- I wonder if you could use more specific language in your hypothesis. What might that sound like?
- You tried one strategy that didn't work, so try something else.
- Way to stick with it. Keep it up.
- Scientists make mistakes.
- You were wrong, so you reviewed your work and tried again. Scientists do that. They try again and again.
- Try explaining that again. I think you mixed up some terminology.

Autonomy

- You've gathered all your materials. Now what might you do?
- What are your thoughts on how to proceed?
- Remember to use what you know.
- You've developed your questions. What's your plan for finding answers?
- I noticed you have written down your hypothesis, but I don't see any rationale. How will you go about providing the rationale for your hypothesis?

It's important to consistently ask students to provide a rationale for their thinking. Doing so creates opportunities for them to deepen their understanding and also supports the development of critical thinking and reasoning. Furthermore, it demonstrates the teacher's belief that students are capable of supporting their ideas and assertions, in this case a hypothesis.

- Based on what you already know, what do you think should be your next step?

Reflection/ Metacognition

- Think about what was difficult for you.
- Write about what you learned about yourself as a scientist.
- How can what you learned today help you in science classes or in life?
- Are there other words you might use to describe what occurred?
- Think about the ways in which you acted and thought like a scientist.
- What can you do if your hypothesis is wrong?

Collaboration

- What do we know?
- You might try discussing this with your partner. Then revise your observation if necessary.
- Talk through what you tried with ______ (student). He or she tried something similar.
- How can we work together to solve this problem?
- Asking clarifying and probing questions is important for scientists because things aren't always what they seem to be or what we expect. Asking your partner these types of questions helps clarify your thinking about what might happen. If you haven't been asking your partner questions, give it a try. Use the question stems if needed.
- Your group looked at all the data and developed some findings. Are you now working on backing up those findings?

Cross-Over

- Scientists need to observe closely, and listening is one aspect of observing. What helped you to listen closely to your partner?
- What will you and your partner do next?
- What questions do you have? How will you find the answers?
- It seems like you are stuck. What do you already know that might help you?
- Take a moment to look at your hypothesis and your data. What do you notice? Does anything surprise you? Take note of patterns, similarities, or differences. Then, share what you noticed with others. Make a list of what you noticed and draw some conclusions.

Notice how the students are doing the heavy lifting? They are synthesizing and analyzing their own data and then working with another pair of students. The classroom structures the teacher has created support a belief that students are capable of deep thinking, their ideas matter, and their thinking supports everyone's learning.

- How's it going? Oh, you thought you decided on a way to organize your conclusions but realized that you had to go back to the data. Scientists do that all the time. They have to continually go back to their data to make sure they aren't misrepresenting anything.

Growth Mindset: Social Studies Comments

In a social studies classroom in which a growth mindset is fostered, time for informal assessments and practice is embedded in the different units. When working on long-term projects, students should receive feedback from the teacher and their peers throughout the process. After an exam, essay, or project is completed, provide students with opportunities to correct misunderstandings. So much of social studies is understanding the validity of sources, examining the perspective and point of view of the author, and seeing individual events within a larger context of cause and effect. Therefore, when planning instruction, remember to provide opportunities for students to explore. In addition, the language you use has the potential to open students' thinking and understanding to different viewpoints and possibilities. Debates and point-counter-point activities should be commonplace, as they require justification and evidence to support claims and opinions. You might also use these comments as students explore social studies topics.

One way to explicitly apply growth mindset understanding is to ask students to identify which mindset they believe a person in history exhibited or what mindset a historical culture/civilization promoted.

Effort/ Resilience

- Figuring out the "truth" can be quite challenging.
- Understanding how decisions have unintended consequences is difficult to fully grasp. Just take it slow and steady.
- I'm not sure everyone understood the pros and cons of ______. If you are unclear, take a few minutes to write what you think you know and then revisit the various texts.
- What you are doing is challenging. It's not easy to find just-right evidence to support a position.

Autonomy

- These are complex ideas. What do you already know that might help you?
- Okay, you've identified a position. What's your plan for supporting your position?
- That is an interesting question. How might you go about finding an answer?
- You've created a calendar for yourself that chunks the project into smaller tasks because you know that is how you learn best.
- Take a few minutes to document what you already know.
- You've made a point and backed it up with evidence from the text, so what's next? Where might your thinking go from here?
- Could you look at the information from a different point of view?

Reflection/ Metacognition

- How did you come to that conclusion?
- How did ______ (student) convince you?
- From whose point of view is this information being told? How might the information change based on a different point of view?
- Reread what you wrote at the beginning of the unit. How has your understanding of ______ changed?
- How does this event relate to ______?
- Based on what you know now, do you think ______ (historical figure) made the right decision?

Collaboration

- ______ (student) had an idea that he/she backed up with evidence from the article. Who can build on that?
- As a group, decide what resources you might need.
- You've pulled from various sources and realized that there is conflicting information. I think ______ (student) came across something similar. Why don't you talk together to come up with a plan for what to do with the conflicting information?
- Apply what you just said to ______'s (student) comment from yesterday.
- Your group wants to argue for ______.

Cross-Over

- You've explained your thinking, but there's still something missing in your rationale, so I'm not sure I'd be swayed to your point of view. Together with your group, go over your thinking process again.
- When I'm struggling to find evidence for a claim I've made, I read over my notes and reflections. That usually helps me find evidence or at least directs me to a resource. I appreciate how reading over my notes gives me a sense of how my idea developed. Does that make sense? Why don't you give that a try.
- Remember, it's a process. You'll have lots of opportunities to revisit your thinking and your piece. When you're working on the piece, your ideas frequently develop and change. That's okay.
- After you've read your notes and reflections, it might help to discuss your progress with ______ (student).
- You don't think that would be the author's stance. But you're not sure why. You could reread the article or talk out some of your ideas.
- As we prepare for our next debate, let's discuss what went well with the last one and what we think we should focus on to improve.

Note that these comments/questions are non-judgmental. They do not include, "I like the way ______ used evidence" or "I love the questions ______ asked." The comments and questions focus on the process of learning and providing students with opportunities to think deeply about topics and events.

Home-School Connections

In a society that promotes fixed mindsets, it is important to provide opportunities in which children understand and internalize that intelligence and talent are malleable—they can be developed. Since most adults grew up in a school system that categorized students as smart or not, it is up to teachers to re-educate parents about the idea that our brains can change and develop with effort and hard work. Even if we are stuck within a system of concrete grades that place a judgment on students' knowledge or understanding, the narrative comments and the way teachers frame their comments to parents can markedly change the way parents perceive their own children. Research has shown that parents' beliefs about success and failure[9] has a great deal to do with children's mindsets. Therefore, when commenting on report cards or speaking with parents informally or during parent-teacher conferences, be sure to include growth mindset comments. Showing parents student work is a great way to guide parents in seeing what students can do and what they know. Sharing and discussing various pieces of work that show progress can also be a great way to illustrate a growth mindset.

Comments for Parents or Guardians

Effort/ Resilience

- _______ (student) asks questions when he/she is faced with a challenge.
- _______ is beginning to understand that we all make mistakes and that it is not only okay, but also important for learning.
- _______ is beginning to understand that explaining his/her thinking not only deepens his or her learning, but also helps others.
- _______ used to avoid sharing mistakes, but now your child is proud to. He/she knows that mistakes help us learn and that sharing our mistakes helps others.
- _______ tries hard to understand different points of view because he/she understands how that will strengthen his/her own understanding.
- _______ knows that if one strategy doesn't work, there are others to try.
- _______ is excited about math now, even though it is difficult, because your child knows that his/her brain is growing.
- _______ understands that with effort and perseverance our brains grow connections. The different connections make us smarter.
- _______ knows that the brain is like a muscle, so for it to get strong, we need to use it. This means he/she has to seek out challenges.

Autonomy

- ______ tries a few things and works out some difficulties before asking for help.
- ______ has developed a system for keeping his/her papers in order, which has really helped your child stay organized.
- ______ is able to synthesize what we are learning by using notes from class discussions and readings.
- ______ comes into class ready. When your child needs a break, he/she puts a slip of paper on my table and takes a walk around the classroom.

Reflection/ Metacognition

- ______ reflects on his/her process and thinks deeply about how he/she can improve.
- ______ thinks about his/her thinking and often asks, "What if…?" which helps him/her see things in new ways.
- It's still difficult for ______ to explain his/her thinking, but your child is working hard at it.
- ______ is able to understand how his/her words or behaviors impact other people.

Collaboration

- ______ listens to other people's ideas and then connects everyone's thinking.
- ______ listens to others in his/her group and accepts when people have different opinions.
- ______ is making an effort to speak up more when working in groups.
- ______ is always willing to share his/her process to help someone who is having difficulty.

Teaching Parents or Guardians About Mindsets

Since so much of our society promotes a fixed mindset, educating parents about a growth mindset and helping parents see how their language can impact their children's understanding of themselves can only support teachers' efforts in the classroom. A few ways to educate parents about the power of a growth mindset include:

- At back-to-school night or other parent gatherings, discuss the different mindsets and ways you will support a growth mindset in the classroom.
- Send home articles and information about perseverance, practice, and mistakes so parents have a sense of what you're working towards in the classroom.
- Engage parents in book clubs about mindsets.
- Share videos and websites about the brain and how it grows when mistakes are made.
- Provide parents with scripts to talk about their child's work.

Final Thoughts

Whether beginning or continuing the journey of developing a classroom that supports a growth mindset, remember that it's a process—one that supports student autonomy, agency, and the ability to work through challenges. This book addressed different aspects of supporting a growth mindset in the classroom, including: recognizing teachers' mindsets, the importance of the classroom environment, the language teachers use, communicating to parents or guardians, and explicitly teaching parents or guardians and students about mindsets. Supporting growth mindsets in the classroom is complex and challenging, so teachers need to give themselves time to work with colleagues and allow themselves to make mistakes. After all, what we learn from our mistakes deepens our resolve and moves us closer to our goal: supporting resilient, independent, and open-minded lifelong learners.

Endnotes/Resources

1 **Dweck, C. S.** (2006). *Mindset: The new psychology of success.* NY: Random House

2 **Dweck, C. S., Walton, G. M. & Cohen, G. L.** (n.d.) Academic tenacity: Mindsets and skills that promote long-term learning. Bill & Melinda Gates Foundation.

3 **Dweck, C. S.** (2017). Growth mindset is on a firm foundation, but we're still building the house. Mindset Scholars Network Blog. Retrieved from http://mindsetscholarsnetwork.org/people/carol-dweck/

4 **Johnston, P. H.** (2012). *Opening Minds.* ME: Stenhouse.

Dweck, C. S. (September 23, 2015). Carol Dweck revisits the 'growth mindset'. *Education Week.*

Goldberg, G. (2015). *Mindsets and moves: Strategies that help readers take charge.* NY: Heinemann.

5 **Kamins, M. L., & Dweck, C. S.** (1999). Person versus process praise and criticism: Implications for contingent self-worth and coping. *Developmental Psychology,* 35(3), 835-847.

6 *Brainology*, https://www.mindsetworks.com/default.

7 **Wilson, J. T., & Montoy-Wilson, M.** (2016). Shift gears to take a growth mindset approach to classroom management. Retrieved from www.mindsetworks.com.

8 **Boaler, J.** (2015). *Mathematical Mindsets.* CA: Jossey-Bass.

9 **Haimovitz, K. & Dweck, C. S.** (2016). Parents' views of failure predict children's fixed and growth mindsets. *Psychological Science,* 27(6), 859-869.

Many thanks to Virginia Dooley for thinking I was the right person to write this series. She knows how near and dear to my heart growth mindset is. Thanks also to Cindy Peattie and Eileen Hillebrand for continuing to work on the project and reigning in my grandiose ideas. And of course, thanks to the teachers I've worked with in the past who have shaped my understanding of teaching and learning. In particular, I'd like to thank Joelle Achilarre, Hannah Jenkins, Shelby Bacchioni, and Eileen Carroll, for reading and offering their expertise and insights on different drafts of this book. Finally, thanks to my dear friend Whitney Bremer for listening to me talk through the organization of the book many times. In the spirit of growth mindset, it certainly was a process.

100+ Growth Mindset Comments

by Rosanne Kurstedt

"I love the concept of this book. I was particularly drawn to the simple shifts in language that could support my students, like using the word "yet" and taking myself out of the feedback. I say, "I like how you ....." a lot. The book is particularly useful because Rosanne gave feedback examples for each subject area. I will definitely place these feedback suggestions in my conference binders for quick reference. The home connection comments are so useful as well. This book should be every teacher's first PD book of the year."

-Bria Cianci, New York City, Elementary School Teacher.

"Kurstedt offers teachers the background, language and tools to seamlessly implement a growth mindset into their classroom repertoire. In return, this approach provides students with invaluable skills and a true understanding of perseverance and effort. I think this book will be one that every teacher will return to again and again. I know I will."

-Joelle Achilarre, Elementary Teacher & Reading Specialist

"Sometimes, I feel challenged and overwhelmed when a student has a rigid defeatist outlook about their abilities to complete challenging tasks. This well-organized book provided me with examples of easy ways to transform both my written and oral language to tackle this challenge. As I read the book I imagined myself using the growth mindset comments while teaching and conferring with students because they were crafted in a way that felt natural and applicable."

-Hannah Jenkins, NYC Public School Teacher (5th Grade)

Also Available!

ABOUT THE AUTHOR

Rosanne Kurstedt is the Associate Director of READ East Harlem/Hunter College and an Adjunct Professor of Education. A former elementary school teacher, she has authored and co-authored numerous professional development books and guides. Rosanne helped establish Hong Kong Academy International School in Hong Kong where she was the Director of Curriculum. In addition, Rosanne writes children's books and in the spring of 2017 founded The Author Experience, a non-profit organization that cultivates the love of story and celebrates the written word by providing author visits, books, and family programming to schools in low-income areas.

Newmark LEARNING
145 Huguenot Street • New Rochelle, NY • 10801

ISBN: 978-1-4788-6130-0
NL4689 9 781478 861300